TOPICAL

SEX, RELATIONSHIPS AND THE BIBLE

Julie Moser

First published January 2004 / Reprinted March 2007
PO Box A287, Sydney South NSW 1235
Tel: 61 2 8268 3344
www.youthworks.net

Scripture quotations taken from the Holy Bible,
New International Version, copyright © 1973, 1978, 1984
by International Bible Society.

ISBN 978-1-876960-86-5
Written by Julie Moser
Edited by Michelle Haines-Thomas
Designed by www.firingminds.com

Introducing Sex, Relationships and the Bible

Dear leader,

You have chosen a set of studies that cover an important topic for young people today. The young person today is bombarded with the world's views on relationships with the opposite sex. These studies are designed to give the young person God's views on relating to the opposite sex. The hope is that they will come to see that living God's way is the better choice.

Be prepared that each young person may be at different stages in regards to relationships. Some may never have had a boyfriend or girlfriend and some may have had many. The group may also have had a wide variety of experiences of relationships especially with issues such as sex, homosexuality, etc. They may also struggle with the fact that their parents are not reflecting God's pattern of relationship outlined in these studies.

Your role as the leader of the young people will vary for each person as you use these studies. For some of the young people your role will be to give them hope that they are not the only one who feels left out in relationship with the opposite sex. For others you may need to urge them to change a current lifestyle that is not in line with God's plan and destructive for them. While still others may need comfort over past regrets and assurance that previous actions are completely forgiven by God when we turn to Christ.

This requires you to be sensitive and open to discuss issues that may arise from these studies. It is very important that you are approachable in regards to the issues raised in discussion. Your support and understanding can give comfort and even healing that the young people may find nowhere else.

I hope these studies will assist you to teach your young people to have the kind of relationships they were designed for, relationships that honour God and, as a result, are healthy for them.

Regards
Julie Moser

Some hints

These studies will work best in a single sex group. The sensitive nature of the topics covered means that the young people may not be able to discuss as openly as they will need to if the opposite sex is present.

If issues are raised that are too difficult for you to handle, speak with your church leader.

It is important that the group feels comfortable to share honestly in the presence of others. For this reason, the young people need to be able to assure each other that there will be no gossip about what is discussed.

It may be helpful for you to ask some of the elders or other wise adults in your church to join you for some or all of these studies. They may be able to contribute in areas where you feel ill-equipped (for example you may be single and not confident to discuss marriage).

Important note

Never promise a young person that you won't tell someone else something that they tell you. These studies may provoke a young person to relate to you situations they are involved in or previously experienced that need some kind of intervention. Some examples are: incest, rape, pregnancy or sexual abuse. In such cases you need to talk with someone in authority such as your minister or a government institution that can deal with these kinds of issues.

BEING IN LOVE

Thinking about what movies, TV and modern songs teach us, what does it mean to be in love?

How are you supposed to feel when you are in love?

What are the good things about being in love?

Do you AGREE or DISAGREE with the statements below?
(Discuss your opinions)
• Being in love is about how you feel.
• Love is permanent.
• You can be in love with two people at the same time.
• Being in love is not always about good times.
• You can 'fall out of love' as easily as you can 'fall in love'
• You have to work at being in love.

1. A strong desire

The book of Song of Songs is about the romantic relationship between two people. **Read the following verses and describe how the couple feel about each other.**

Song of Songs 1:15-16

Song of Songs 3:1-4

Do you think being in love always starts with a strong desire?

2. Strong desire that leads to a commitment

The strong desire of romantic love does not last forever. It changes into something deeper as a couple gets to know each other better. We know that the strong desire is more than just a feeling when it leads to something permanent. **What do the following verses teach us about the commitment of love?**

Song of Songs 8:5-7

Genesis 29:14–20

The greatest example of love in the Bible is demonstrated by God's love for us.
Read John 3:16, 1 John 4:10 and John 15:13.
How is God's love different from some popular views about what love is?

How can we show the same kind of love for the person we are 'in love' with?

From today's study, how can two people know they are 'in love'?

GOING OUT (DATING)

What do you think is the best age to start going out with someone?
Choose an age group below and then discuss the positives and negatives of going out with someone at that age:

UP TO AGE 11 ☐   12-14 ☐   15-16 ☐   17 ☐   18-20 ☐   21 AND ABOVE ☐

Do you AGREE or DISAGREE with the statements below?
(Discuss your opinions):
• It is OK to go out with someone and flirt with someone else.
• It is OK to go out with lots of people one after the other.
• It is OK to have sex with the person you are going out with 'if you love them'.
• You only go out with someone you plan to marry.

GOD'S INSTRUCTIONS FOR HEALTHY RELATIONSHIPS

The Bible doesn't talk about going out (dating) because people didn't date each other in Bible times – they had arranged marriages! We do know, however, that the Bible has a great deal to teach us about how to have good relationships.
What do the following passages teach us about good relationships?

Philippians 2:3-4

Colossians 3:12-14

This passage talks about showing restraint physically.
Discuss: how 'far can you go' (physically) when you are not married?

Make a list to describe the perfect Christian couple – how would they behave?

CHRISTIANS DATING CHRISTIANS

Read about Solomon, king of Israel: 1 Kings 11:1-6.
What was Solomon's big mistake? (see especially verse 4)

What lessons can we learn from this story about the danger of having a relationship with someone who doesn't share our faith?

Although people in Bible times had arranged marriages, the widow (someone whose wife/husband has died) was allowed to choose their own partner if they wanted to re-marry. Read 1 Corinthians 7:39.
Who was a Christian widow to choose?

We live in a society that is free to choose our own partners. **What are the advantages in a Christian choosing a partner who is also a Christian?**

Discuss the following issues that can arise when going out with someone:
• There is a temptation to go too far sexually.
• Sometimes couples only spend time with each other and exclude other friends.
• When you break up it can fracture your group of friends/youth group.

GROUP ADVICE

Try to come up with three pieces of good advice about 'going out':

Sample Advice:
When you under 18, try to resist going out too early. Work at building up a good group of friends who can care for each other and enjoy each other's company.

Advice 1:

Advice 2:

Advice 3:

SEX

If you were to sum up your society's view on sex in one sentence, what would it be?

Do you AGREE or DISAGREE with the statements below?
(Discuss your opinions)

• Sex is for when you are in love.
• It doesn't matter who you have sex with as long as it is safe sex (using a condom).
• It is acceptable these days to have sex with someone who is the same sex as you.
• Going too far sexually with your girlfriend/boyfriend is unforgiveable.

GOD IS POSITIVE ABOUT SEX

People think that the Christian faith is 'anti-sex'. However the Bible is clear that God created sex to be a great experience when used in the special relationship it was created for.

One of the first commands to people was to have sex (increase in number). **Read Genesis 1:27-28.**

Married couples are encouraged to have sex. **Read 1 Corinthians 7:3-5.**

The entire book of Song of Songs in the Old Testament is about the love between a man and woman, including having sex.

Why do you think people consider the Christian faith as being 'against sex'?

GOD SETS LIMITS ON SEX

While God created sex to be enjoyed, he also set limits on sex.
The Bible outlaws:

- **Incest** (sex with close relatives). Leviticus 18:6 (and verses 7–18)
- **Homosexuality** (same sex relationships). Romans 1:18 and 26–27
- **Beastiality** (sex with animals). Exodus 22:19
- **Adultery** (sex where one or both people are married to someone else). Exodus 20:14
- **Sex with someone you are not married to.** Hebrews 13:4 and Romans 13:13

Can you see reasons for the limits set by God in the list above?

Sex is great when it is within a marriage relationship as God designed.
**Compare the situations of sex in marriage and sex outside marriage.
What advantages can you see in having sex within marriage?**

CHOOSE THE BETTER LIFESTYLE

Read 1 Corinthians 6:12–20.
What reasons does this passage give us for keeping sex within marriage?

Read 1 Thessalonians 4:3–7.
**What does this passage say to the person who believes sex outside
marriage doesn't hurt anyone?**

Read Ephesians 5:1–3 and Colossians 3:1–7.
How is the Christian to be different from everyone else?

Important note
God forgives us when we mess up and removes sin and guilt.
Read Colossians 1:21–22.

NOTES

MARRIAGE

What are some good reasons to get married?

What are some bad reasons to get married?

What do you think the perfect age to get married is? Why?

Do you AGREE or DISAGREE with the statements below?
(Discuss your opinions)

• Living together is the same as being married.

• A Christian marriage has a better chance at lasting.

• Most people don't take their marriage vows (promises) seriously.

WHAT DOES GOD SAY ABOUT MARRIAGE?

Below are some verses that say some general things about marriage.
• Genesis 2:19-24
• 1 Corinthians 7:1-2
• 1 Corinthians 7:8-9
• 1 Corinthians 7:10-11
• Proverbs 18:22 and Proverbs 19:14

Why do you think some marriages don't last?

THE MARRIAGE VOWS

What promises do two people make when they marry?
Read the marriage vows below.

• *X, will you take Y to be your wife, to live together according to God's law? Will you give her the honour due to her as your wife and, forsaking all others, love and protect her, as long as you both shall live? I will*
(This is repeated by the wife)

• *I X, in the presence of God, take you Y to be my wife; to have and to hold from this day forward, for better for worse, for richer for poorer, in sickness and in health, to love and to cherish, as long as we both shall live. This is my solemn vow and promise.*
(This is repeated by the wife)

Think through the implications of the marriage promises and give some examples of circumstances in which you would need to keep these marriage vows. For example sickness and in health – your partner becomes crippled.

We must be very careful about making promises to someone unless we believe we can keep them. Read what God says about making promises in Ecclesiastes 5:5.

What do you think is the hardest promise to make from the marriage vows?

Is worried they will never get married?

Is afraid of marriage because they have seen failure in their own families?

Believes that divorce is OK if you don't love them anymore?

THE PARTNERSHIP OF MARRIAGE

5

To make a marriage work, what are some things a couple needs to do?

Do you AGREE or DISAGREE with the statements below?
(Discuss your opinions)
• In a Christian marriage the husband makes all the decisions.
• The husband must always control the budget (money).
• God designed marriage as an equal partnership.
• A husband is allowed to boss his wife around.

A BIBLICAL MODEL OF A MARRIAGE PARTNERSHIP

Read Ephesians 5:22-33 and 1 Peter 3:1-7.
What is the wife to do for her husband?

What is the husband to do for his wife?

How will this commitment by both people make a strong marriage?

The Wife
Some people react negatively to the idea of a wife submitting to her husband.
Many consider the word submit to be the same as the word 'obey'. However
if you read about the relationship of children to parents (Ephesians 6:1) and
slaves to masters (Ephesians 6:5) you see the word 'obey' used. Paul makes

a distinction between the relationship of slaves and masters/children and parents to the partnership of a husband and wife.

If 'submit' does not mean 'obey', what do you think it means that the wife should 'submit' to her husband?

Can you think of some examples of submission?

The submissive wife is often pictured as a weak downtrodden woman. The Bible gives an example of a good wife in the book of Proverbs. Read Proverbs 31:10-31. **What kind of wife is she? What kinds of activities is she involved in?**

How does her example destroy the image of the weak downtrodden woman?

From the Bible a good wife is:

The Husband
There seems to be much more responsibility by the husband than the wife. The example of Christ and the church shows that the husband is to lay down his life for his wife.